PEAR TREE

Kalwinder Si

A love letter of sorts and thoughts to the city of Derby and it's wonderful folk.

A collection of poetry and prose, which follows the life of a Derby boy. Touching upon identity, community, culture and many other things that define and strengthen the man that he has become.

WARNING: May contain words that some people find offensive.

Cover design by Kalwinder Singh Dhindsa

Edited by Fine Point Editing

@FP_Editing
www.finepointediting

Copyright © 2018 by Kalwinder Singh Dhindsa

All rights reserved

The right of Kalwinder Singh Dhindsa to be identified as the author of this work has been asserted by him in accordance with the Copyright, Designs and Patents Act, 1988.

This book or any portion thereof may not be reproduced or used in any manner whatsoever without the express written permission of the publisher except for the use of brief quotations in a book review.

ISBN: 9781731395764

@KhalSir
@PearTreeDerby
www.khalsir.com

"Derby County Football Club provided me with the platform to honour my father"

Kalwinder Singh Dhindsa

October 2018

CONTENTS

01. Pardon My French.
02. Total ReKal.
03. Falsehood.
04. Fud.
05. Sikh.
06. Honour Thy Pigeon.
07. Mind Your Language.
08. Tainted.
09. Bully.
10. Heartbeat.
11. Derby.
12. Defiance.
13. An Abode to Alf Quantrill.
14. Code Der Stille.
15. Community.
16. First – Born.
17. Playscheme.
18. Alter Ego.
19. Suffragist.
20. Kevin Coyne.
21. Sikh Poppy Khanda.
22. He/Art.
23. Bliss.
24. Paki.
25. Samosa.

ABOUT THE AUTHOR
ACKNOWLEDGEMENTS
BOOKS

01. Pardon My French.

Born in Derby - 1979

British Punjabi of Sikh origine.

Raised with a topknot, my Mother's decree.

A misunderstood child. Es-tu une fille?

Proud of my roots and all things Punjabi.

A Doctor Who loving Sikh Derby boy - Toujours Pear Tree.

02. Total ReKal.

A **recalcitrant** is what you are.

No I am not, I beg to differ.

adjective

having an obstinately uncooperative attitude towards authority or discipline.

A **recalcipotent** is what you see.

Show me a good leader and I shall be devoted to thee.

adjective

having an obstinately uncooperative attitude towards incompetence hiding behind authority.

03. Falsehood.

Look at me!

Can't you see!

I'm better than anything you'll ever be.

For I wear a cloak of respectability.

These garments I wear are my refuge.

Thou shall not question my subterfuge.

04. Fud.

A fud. A fud. That's what you are.

A joy sapper, a weasel a ball breaker.

I have no desire to be drunk or get smashed.

I am comfortable stone sober unabashed.

Please leave me alone I am what I am.

The old boy from Pear Tree forever a Ram.

05. Sikh.

I am Sikh. Topknot I mourn.

Hair cut short perpetually shorn.

Roots not lost to be forgot.

I am Sikh like it or knot.

06. Honour Thy Pigeon.

Rats with wings not pretty little things.

Disgusting and diseased nothing but mings.

Feral and free they have no respect.

Eyes on your food or maybe your neck?

Related to doves and racing royalty.

32 Dickin Medals for war time gallantry.

I am from Derby just like the blue cock.

A legend of flight that we should not mock.

Blue Cork of West Derby you must come and see'em.

Rests with Wrights in Derby Museum.

The King of Rome; glass box on a wall.

The pride of Derby; loved by all.

07. Mind Your Language.

'Commit suicide' connotes a crime.

My father was no criminal he did not serve time.

Please adopt 'died by' instead of 'commit'.

Think of the bereaved it does not befit.

Words can be dangerous and damage the mind.

Choose them more wisely it's good to be kind.

08. Tainted.

Normanton Derby Sikh born and raised.

You're not fit to police and we suspect ill behaved.

Stuff your job you manipulative crook.

This Pear Tree man is off the hook.

Community first and never reject.

Jog on you chief I shall not forget.

09. Bully.

"Break their ******* legs" a voice ascends.

I'm not having that I must make amends.

"Hold your heads high my brave little boys"

Ignore the foul mouth and his incessant noise.

"There's no need for that", I approach with a grin.

"**** off you ****. I'll smash your face in".

What a big baby. What a sore loser.

My young boys just defeated a bruiser.

10. Heartbeat.

Boro born and Redcar raised.

A Stainsby girl from Acklam Grange.

My wife to be my new fiancé.

From the land of Clough and Rea's Cafe.

11. Derby.

Derby, England my home city.

Rolls-Royce aero factory.

Merlin engines that won the war.

"Produced in Osmaston" Hear us roar !

Derby folk in dignity.

'46 abide with me.

Charlton beaten. Wembley.

Rams victorious - D.C.F.C.

12. Defiance.

Stand firm. Strike hard. Do not submit.

Resist like a tiger. The Khalsa spirit.

The Punjabi farmer. They call him Victoria.

The Naik from Nawanshahr. A legend. A warrior.

A man of steel with limitless courage.

Gian Singh V.C of Sahabpur Village.

13. An Abode to Alf Quantrill.

English blood Punjabi heart.

The boy from Rawalpindi to England depart.

Signed by Derby County in 1914.

Division One promotion in 1915.

A call to arms. Derbyshire Yeomanry.

Struck down with malaria. Sent back to Blighty.

Capped by England in 1920.

In the footsteps of a legend in-law to be.

Steve Bloomer of England and Derby County.

The father of Hetty, Mrs Quantrill to be.

First of the Punjabi Rams of Derby.

Alf Quantrill's abode. The boy from Rawalpindi.

14. Code Der Stille.

A Headmaster from The Bemrose School.

Raymond Chapman born to rule.

A Doctor in Philosophy.

Cloaked in deepest secrecy.

Secrets Act declassify.

Raymond Chapman was not a spy.

Bletchley Park the Ultra abode.

Cracking Nazi Enigma code.

Fluent in German. Innsbruck PhD

Raymond Chapman found the key.

15. Community.

English heart Punjabi blood.

Normanton. My neighbourhood.

Children born of foreigners.

Immigrants from all corners.

This is Derby we shall roam.

Until the end. It is our home.

16. First - Born.

What's y'name Sir?

Mr Singh.

Where y'from Sir?

Derby.

No! Where y'born Sir?

The City Hospital.

Where's that Sir?

Derby.

Here Sir?!

Yes. I'm a Derby Man.

17. Playscheme.

Six weeks off. Summer holidays await.

Back to School don't jump the gate.

All doors open, kids rush in.

Andy's here. Thank God, Amen.

Football, pool, trips and games.

He keeps us safe. Knows all our names.

Thirty years later I wish to say.

Andy 'The King' Robert Bruce of Pear Tree.

Thank You always. R.I.P.

18. Alter Ego.

Marion Elizabeth Adnams.

First art mistress of Homelands.

English painter, draughtswoman and printmaker.

Surrealist artist. Dream-like vision creator.

Paintings reminiscent of Nash, Magritte and Dali.

The mistress of art. Born in Derby.

19. Suffragist.

Supporter of suffrage and anti-war.

The people of Derby know the score.

A Blue Plaque and Star. Rightly bestowed.

Alice Ann Wheeldon of Pear Tree Road.

20. Kevin Coyne.

Ey Up Me Duck.

On guitar he would pluck.

Blues he could sing.

The original punk king.

An artist, a musician, a singer.

A composer, a poet, a painter.

A writer and film maker.

The anti-star mental health crusader.

21. Sikh Poppy Khanda.

A trip to Alrewas NMA.

To pay respect. Remembrance Day.

A glance at a table poppy display.

Where are my Sikhs?. I ask in dismay.

A gut wrenching feeling of emptiness.

I can't let this go. I must address.

To honour my people of the Punjab region.

I design a Poppy Khanda for the Royal British Legion.

22. He/Art.

Impossible dreams he did avoke.

Andy Edwards the man from Stoke.

Get down here fast and leave your mark.

Steve Bloomer's watching at Pride Park.

Derby County's revered icons.

Sculpt in clay and cast in bronze

The boy from Pear Tree he did take part.

Your broken heart he turned to art.

23. Bliss.

What's that Dad up in the air?

Curious, interested and aware.

It's a rainbow high in the blue.

Happiness as light shines through.

24. Paki.

Man with beard and brown skin.

"Mr Khan". They laugh and grin.

Silly little fools without a clue.

Laughing at me is laughing at you.

Show some respect and observe our faces.

We're all Pakis to ignorant racists.

25. Samosa.

Takes me home in flashback.

Triangular entrée. Punjabi snack.

ABOUT THE AUTHOR

Born in Derby in 1979,

Kalwinder Singh Dhindsa attended Village
Community School – a short walk from his childhood
home in Pear Tree. He then graduated from the University
of Leicester with an Honours Degree in Physics with
Astrophysics followed by a PGCE Secondary
Physics.
These days he
works as a science technician
at Littleover Community School.
Life-long member of the Derby Civic Society.

ACKNOWLEDGEMENTS

Thank You

BOOKS

My Father & The Lost Legend of Pear Tree - Part One (2016)

Punjabi Alphabet Activity Book (2016)

Homelands Revisited (2017)

Punjabi Number Activity Book (2017)

Punjabi Exercise Book (2017)

Punjabi Activity Book (2017)

My Father & The Lost Legend of Pear Tree - Part Two (2018)

The Colour of Madness: Exploring BAME mental health in the UK (2018)

Pear Tree Rambler (2018)

Pear Tree Rampage (2019)

Printed in Poland
by Amazon Fulfillment
Poland Sp. z o.o., Wrocław